The Danger

DICK FRANCIS

Level 4

Retold by John Escott
Series Editor: Derek Strange

PENGUIN BOOKS

PENGUIN BOOKS

Published by the Penguin Group
Penguin Books Ltd, 27 Wrights Lane, London W8 5TZ, England
Penguin Books USA Inc., 375 Hudson Street, New York, New York 10014, USA
Penguin Books Australia Ltd, Ringwood, Victoria, Australia
Penguin Books Canada Ltd, 10 Alcorn Avenue, Toronto, Ontario, Canada M4V 3B2
Penguin Books (NZ) Ltd, 182–190 Wairau Road, Auckland 10, New Zealand

Penguin Books Ltd, Registered Offices: Harmondsworth, Middlesex, England

The Danger © Dick Francis 1983
This adaptation published by Penguin Books 1993
4 6 8 10 9 7 5 3

Text copyright © John Escott 1993
Illustrations copyright © Chris Chaisty (David Lewis Illustrators) 1993
All rights reserved

The moral right of the adapter and of the illustrator has been asserted

Illustrations by Chris Chaisty (David Lewis Illustrators)

Printed in England by Clays Ltd, St Ives plc
Set in 11/13pt Lasercomp Bembo

To the teacher:

In addition to all the language forms of Levels One to Three, which are used again at this level of the series, the main verb forms and tenses used at Level Four are:

- present perfect continuous verbs, past perfect verbs, *was/were going to*, passive verbs (simple aspects only and with available modal verbs), conditional clauses (using the 'second' or 'improbable' or 'hypothetical future' conditional) and further phrasal verbs

- modal verbs: *should* and *ought to* (to give advice or expressing desirability), *used to* (to describe past habits, states and routines), *must* and *can't* (to express deduced likelihood), *may* and *might* (to express possibility or uncertainty), *could* (to express hypothetical ability), *would* (to express willingness) and *had better* (to give advice).

Specific attention is paid to vocabulary development in the Vocabulary Work exercises at the end of the book. These exercises are aimed at training students to enlarge their vocabulary systematically through intelligent reading and effective use of a dictionary.

To the student:

Dictionary Words
- As you read this book, you will find that some words are in darker black ink than the others on the page. Look them up in your dictionary, if you do not already know them, or try to guess the meaning of the words first, and then look them up later, to check.

PART ONE: ITALY

Chapter One

It all went wrong in Bologna. I stood as still as possible in the back of the ambulance, my whole body cold with anger, and watched. **Carabinieri* officers** burst from the dark corners of the street and into the silence of the summer night – voices shouting, hands waving guns. There was so much confusion they didn't see the two men with the suitcase full of money – £650,000. They were more interested in the young man falling out of the other car. He had brought the **ransom** money. Now he was shot, and I saw the dark red blood on his shirt.

The two men ran to a hidden car and drove away.

Alessia Cenci was twenty-three. She had been with the kidnappers for five weeks, three days and ten hours – and she had never been closer to death than now, I thought.

It was not a real ambulance I was inside, it was a van. Inside its darkly painted windows were a lot of small machines. One of them was telling us where the suitcase and the money were going. It was receiving sounds from something we had put inside the suitcase. We followed it to some flats and stopped. In front of the building was a black car, its engine cooling. Police cars stopped and parked, their doors open and lights shining brilliantly across the street.

◆

At midnight, Enrico Pucinelli arrived.

'I am controlling things now,' he said. 'The kidnappers are in the front apartment on the third floor and they say they have kidnapped the people who live there and will kill them if we don't let them go. They say Alessia Cenci will die, too.' He looked at

---

* *Carabinieri*. The name for the Italian police.

me. 'My men say you wanted to let the kidnappers get away, taking the money with them.'

'Yes,' I said.

'They shot the boy who drove the car,' he said. 'We can't let them escape now.'

'The boy knew it was dangerous. The girl must still be saved.'

I was still angry. The boy was shot because the local police tried to catch the men when they came for the suitcase of money. He was supposed to leave the money in the car and walk away, but the carabinieri did not give him that chance.

'Is he still alive?' I asked.

'I don't know,' said Pucinelli. 'He's gone to the hospital.'

Liberty Market, the company I worked for, was not going to be pleased. It was my job to end a kidnap in a quiet way, and with no trouble. My job to make sure the **victim** stayed safe. But what about Alessia Cenci, one of the best woman **jockeys** in the world? Could I bring her home safely now?

'Advise me,' said Pucinelli. 'It's your job.'

'Phone the kidnappers and tell them you're arranging things and they must wait. It will help to calm things down if you take some time.'

He did this from the van, and I listened. I didn't understand every word of his Italian because he spoke too quickly, but the kidnappers soon stopped shouting at the other end of the phone.

Outside in the street, a crowd of people watched. Newspaper reporters mixed with children and women from other flats. One man was near the ambulance, holding two cameras but not taking photographs. His head was round, he had black hair, and he was wearing a leather jacket. A newspaper reporter, I thought.

The telephone in the van rang suddenly. Pucinelli picked it up and listened. The kidnappers were getting nervous and didn't want to wait any longer. They wanted the police to let them go safely to the airport, and they wanted an aeroplane waiting there to fly them out.

Outside in the street, a crowd of people watched. Newspaper reporters mixed with children and women from other flats.

Pucinelli put down the phone. 'There'll be no aeroplane.'

'Do as they say,' I said. 'You can catch them when the girl is home.'

'No,' he said. 'I can't make that decision.'

'Talk to someone who can,' I said. 'I'm going back to the Villa Francese.'

Somewhere in or near the city, a young woman was in great danger. The two kidnappers in the flat were only the two who had come for the money. There were others. And one of them was the man who gave the orders. The man I called HIM.

Chapter Two

Alessia's father, Paolo Cenci, was waiting at the Villa Francese. His wife was dead so Alessia had no mother to worry about her, but Paolo Cenci worried enough for two people.

'Andrew! What happened?' he wanted to know. 'Giorgio Traventi phoned to say his son was shot.' His face was grey, his eyes wide with fear. 'Nobody has told me anything. I've been waiting for five hours!'

He was fifty-six and a strong man, but his voice was shaking as he spoke. I told him everything that had happened, and he sat with his head in his hands and listened.

'They'll kill her,' he said after I stopped speaking.

The telephone next to him rang. Nervously, he picked it up.

'Ricardo? Yes, I understand,' he said. 'I will come now.'

'Was that Ricardo Traventi?' I asked. 'Lorenzo's brother?'

'Yes, but I must go alone,' he said.

'No, I'll drive you.' I was working as his driver. His real driver was taking a holiday. 'What did Ricardo say?'

'The kidnappers telephoned. Ricardo says he must meet us at the usual place.' Cenci was already moving towards the door and I followed him.

The kidnappers telephoned the Traventis' house because they knew the police listened to the phone calls at Paolo Cenci's house. Giorgio Traventi was a lawyer and he took the kidnappers' messages. The whole Traventi family wanted to help, and his son, Lorenzo Traventi, had wanted to take the ransom money. Now the boy was in hospital.

I drove Cenci to meet Ricardo. The meeting place – a motorway restaurant – was HIS choice. At four o'clock in the morning the motorway was quiet, and Ricardo was waiting in the restaurant car park.

'Lorenzo is seriously ill, Papa says,' Ricardo said angrily.

'I'm very sorry,' said Paolo Cenci. ' But what is the message?'

'To stand by the telephones.'

'Was it the same man?' I asked.

'I think so. He said Signor Cenci must be alone, and that if there were any more carabinieri, we wouldn't see Alessia again.'

Cenci was shaking.

'I'll stay in the car,' I said. 'Don't be afraid.'

He walked to the entrance of the restaurant, not looking back.

Ricardo and I waited, not speaking much, and I began to fear that no phone call would come. Cenci came back as the sky was getting lighter.

'He says Alessia is alive, but the price has gone up,' he said. 'I must pay two thousand million lire in two days, and if anyone tells the carabinieri about the new price, Alessia will die immediately.' He looked at Ricardo. 'You must say nothing. Promise me.'

Ricardo, looking serious, promised.

We returned to the villa.

'Do you think we'll get her back?' asked Cenci.

There were pictures of Alessia, the famous girl jockey, in most rooms of the house. I'd never met her, but I'd read about her in the newspapers. 'Yes,' I said. 'The kidnappers don't want to kill her.'

Tears began to run down Cenci's face. With them ran some of the fear, sadness and anger inside him, and I said nothing. We sat for half an hour drinking cognac, then he went to get ready to go to his office.

Chapter Three

I drove Cenci to his office, then went to the flats. The carabinieri's cars and the dark-windowed ambulance were still in the street. A small crowd watched quietly, but everything seemed calm. I pretended not to be too interested because I didn't know who was watching me. After a few minutes I went to find a telephone and I phoned the number of the ambulance. I asked to speak to Enrico Pucinelli.

'Andrew?' his voice said a moment later. 'Nothing's changed. My bosses can't make a decision about the aeroplane. Talk, talk, talk!'

'What are the kidnappers saying?'

'The same. The girl will die if they don't get away safely.'

'Did they talk to anybody during the night?' I said. 'By radio?'

'You think they have a radio? Why do you think that?'

'I thought they might speak to the people keeping Alessia,' I said carefully. I wanted to know if HE knew what was going on.

'What are you not telling me?' said Pucinelli.

Cenci wanted me to keep quiet about the new ransom, and Cenci was paying me. 'Nothing,' I said.

◆

Two days later, Cenci got all the ransom money from his bank.

'I have to go back to the motorway restaurant, tomorrow morning at eight,' he said. 'I have to take the money in my car and wait for him ... for his orders. He'll be angry if I have a driver.'

'Tell him you never drive. And tell him you need to be sure Alessia is alive.'

We drove away from the villa with the money in the back of the car. The traffic was light and we arrived at the restaurant half an hour early. Cenci jumped out of the car and walked across to the entrance. A few minutes later, somebody knocked on the car window next to me. It was a man in a white shirt and a leather jacket, and he was asking me to open the window.

'Who are you waiting for?' he said.

'Signor Cenci,' I said.

'Not Count Rieti?'

'No. Sorry.'

'You're not Italian?' the man said.

'No,' I said. 'I'm from Andalucia in Spain.'

'It's very hot there now,' he said in careful Spanish.

'Yes,' I said. I could speak Spanish and knew Andalucia well.

'Do you always drive for Signor ... Cenci?'

'Yes,' I said. 'He never drives a car himself.'

'Why not?' asked the man.

'I don't know,' I said. 'He always has somebody to drive for him.'

I pretended to lose interest in the conversation and he walked away. I looked carefully at him – the round shape of his head, his black hair, and his leather jacket – *and I knew I had seen him before.* He had been outside the ambulance, near the flats. I had thought he was a newspaper reporter then. Now I knew this meeting was no strange accident.

He knew my face now. Did he believe I was just a Spanish driver? I thought he probably did, or I'd be sitting there with a knife in my back.

It was after nine o'clock when Cenci came back.

'Where are we to go?' I started the car engine.

'To Mazara, twenty kilometres south. Another restaurant, another telephone, in twenty minutes. I heard Alessia's voice, on a cassette. She's alive, because she was reading today's newspaper. But if anything goes wrong this time, he'll kill her.'

The day was becoming warm. The roads were narrow and

13

straight, with fields on each side. No car followed us. At Mazara, Cenci went to the café and I stayed with the car. I watched him sitting at a table, staring at a cup of coffee. Suddenly, he jumped up and went across to a phone.

A few minutes after this, he came back to the car and got inside.

'He says…' He tried to make his voice calm. 'He says there's a sort of **shrine** near the road we came along.'

I nodded. 'I saw it.'

I started the car and drove away from the café. We drove ten kilometres, and there by the road side was a simple stone shrine. It was just a wall about two metres high, with a **Madonna** in front of it. Rain had washed most of the blue paint from the Madonna.

We took the box from the car and carried it to the back of the shrine.

Two thousand million lire. Almost a million pounds.

Chapter Four

We waited the rest of that day and all day Sunday. Cenci seemed to become thinner as each hour passed. At eleven o'clock on Monday morning, there was a phone call. Cenci listened, looked confused by the things he heard, then put the phone down.

'Something about my things being ready, and to go and get them,' he said. 'Do you think …?'

'I don't know. Was it the same voice?' Cenci was not certain. 'Well, let's try,' I said. 'It's better than sitting here.'

'But where? He didn't say.'

'Perhaps the place we left the ransom money.' I saw hope come into his face. 'Don't be too hopeful. He may mean somewhere different.'

I drove fast, but it seemed a lifetime to him. And when we stopped by the shrine, there was nothing to be seen except for the Madonna.

'Oh no … oh no!' Cenci's voice was breaking. 'I can't …'

'Wait,' I said, getting out of the car.

I walked round to the back of the shrine ... and found her there. She was asleep and was wearing no clothes, except for a grey plastic coat.

♦

We took her back to the villa and I phoned Pucinelli at the ambulance.

'She's home,' I said.

'Alessia?' said Pucinelli. He sounded unable to believe it.

'She's **drugged** but not harmed. Don't hurry, she'll probably sleep for hours. How are things down there?'

'Andrew!' Now he sounded annoyed. 'What's been going on?'

'Will you come here yourself?' I said.

'Yes,' he said, and put down the phone.

But ten minutes later, he phoned back.

'Things are happening here,' he said. 'Come down, if you want to.'

I went as quickly as possible.

'One of the kidnappers telephoned here,' Pucinelli told me when I arrived. 'In twenty minutes one of them will come out with the mother and baby from the flat. He'll have no gun. If we take him peacefully, one of the children will leave, followed by the father. If the second kidnapper is sure he'll be safe, he'll come out with the second child.'

'They telephoned you very soon after Alessia was home,' I said.

'I suspect they knew,' said Pucinelli.

'Yes. We suspected they were getting orders from someone.'

'A radio message,' I said. 'You'll look for the radio?'

'What are they going to do with the money?' I asked.

'They'll leave it in the flat,' Pucinelli told me.

The woman and baby came out first, the woman covering her eyes from the brilliant light of the sun. She was followed by a young man who walked from the flats with his hands above his head.

'Lie down on the road!' Pucinelli told him. 'You will not be shot.'

There was a long, hold-your-breath quiet. Then a boy of about six came out. His mother waved madly to him through the window of the police car, and he ran across. Soon after, another man walked out into the street. His hands were tied behind his back and he stopped and looked at the kidnapper on the road. He seemed unable to move, so Pucinelli went across and brought him back to the cars. After this, it was quiet for a long time and I began to think things were going wrong. In the end, Pucinelli bravely took his gun and went into the flats alone.

There were no sounds of shooting, but suddenly there was somebody by the door; a big man carrying a little girl on one arm. Behind him came Pucinelli. The policeman pointed to the other kidnapper on the road, and the big man put down the little girl and got down beside him.

It was finished. We found the ransom money under a bed in the flat. The radio was in a kitchen cupboard, and their guns were by the window.

'You were lucky he didn't shoot you in the street,' I said.

'I didn't think he would,' Pucinelli said calmly. 'But when I was coming up the stairs, I did begin to wonder whether ...' He half-smiled, gave me a friendly nod and left.

I telephoned Liberty Market in London.

'The girl's home,' I told them. 'Two of the kidnappers are with the police and the first ransom money is safe.'

They wanted to know when I was coming back to London.

'Two or three days, if I think the girl is going to be OK,' I said.

Chapter Five

Next morning, Pucinelli came to talk to Alessia. 'Please tell us what happened, from the beginning,' he said.

She looked weak and tired after her drugged sleep. 'I ... it

16

seems so long ago. I'd been **racing** on our local **racecourse** and I'd won the six o'clock **race**. I was driving home, thinking of England, and of riding Brunelleschi in the Derby*.' She stopped, then said, 'Did he win?'

'No,' I said. 'He was fourth.'

'Oh.' She returned to her story. 'I was here, not far from the gate, and I slowed down to turn in. There was a car coming towards me and I waited for it to pass, but it stopped suddenly, between me and the gate. The doors opened and four men jumped out. They were wearing **masks**, and I thought they wanted to rob me, but they jumped into my car. They were so quick … they put a bag over my head … and it made me go to sleep … they were lifting me out of the car. Then, nothing … until I woke up in a tent, in a room. A man was next to me, hitting my face. He wore a mask and he made me say some words, then I went back to sleep.'

We all knew the words. We had listened to them many times, on the first cassette the kidnappers sent : *'This is Alessia. Please do as they say. They will kill me if you don't.'*

'Could you see the room outside the tent?' asked Pucinelli.

'No.'

'Could you hear anything?'

'Only music on a cassette. Verdi's *Il Trovatore* – again and again.'

'Can you remember anything more?'

She looked at the floor. Her face looked thin and very tired now. 'They gave me things from newspapers to read aloud, and told me to say something which happened when I was a child. Something only my father knew about. "Then he'll know you're alive," they said.'

'Did you see a microphone?' asked Pucinelli.

'No. I suppose it was outside the tent.'

'Can you remember their voices?'

She began to shake. 'Two of them, yes.'

* *the Derby*. A famous English horse race.

The doors opened and four men jumped out. They were wearing masks, and I thought they wanted to rob me.

'If we play you a cassette they sent to your father, can you tell us if you recognize the man's voice?'

'Oh … yes, of course.'

Cenci held his daughter's hand while they listened.

'Cenci. We have your daughter, Alessia. We will return her after you pay us one hundred and fifty thousand million lire. If you do not pay, we will kill her. Do not delay. Do not inform the carabinieri or we will hurt her …'

Pucinelli stopped the voice before it said more terrible things. Alessia was shaking badly and was finding it difficult to speak. But she was nodding. 'Yes … Papa, you didn't pay all that money?'

'Don't worry,' Cenci told her.

'Did they move you to another place four or five days ago?' I asked.

She shook her head, but then started to wonder whether she was right. 'I was in that tent all the time. But the last few days there was the smell of bread cooking, and the light was better. But I slept so much …'

'Do you think you slept while they moved you to another place?'

'Perhaps. There was one day I slept a lot, and when I woke up, I felt sick, like I did yesterday.' She turned to her father and held him close to her. 'I'm so glad to be here, Papa. I'm so grateful …'

He touched her hair and his eyes filled with tears.

Pucinelli chose that moment to leave and I went outside with him.

'She knows very little,' he said. 'The kidnappers were too careful.'

'I can help you make a picture of one of the other kidnappers.'

'How? Where did you see him?' Pucinelli looked very surprised.

'I've seen him twice,' I said, and explained about the man near the ambulance. 'I saw him again outside the motorway restaurant.'

We went to Pucinelli's office and he got an artist to come in. We began to make a picture of the man.

'He's about thirty, probably,' I said. The artist started to draw a picture of a face and I looked at it. 'His head is rounder, his mouth thinner.' I described as much as I remembered, and slowly the picture began to look like the man.

'I'll show this to the kidnappers who were in the flats,' said Pucinelli. 'They are refusing to say anything about the kidnap, but this will shock them.'

I hoped he was right.

PART TWO: ENGLAND

Chapter Six

Two days later, I went back to London – and Alessia came with me.

'I'm going to stay with Popsy,' she told her father. Popsy was a woman **racehorse trainer** in England.

'Why must you go?' argued Cenci. 'There are horses here.'

'Papa, I want to go away. It's wonderful to be home, but … I tried to drive my car out of the gate today, and I was shaking. It was stupid. I'll go with Andrew, if he doesn't mind.'

I didn't mind at all.

On the aeroplane, Alessia said, 'Popsy lives in Lambourn.' She paused, then went on, 'I want to keep on seeing you.'

I nodded. She was pretty, and I was starting to like her more and more.

At the airport in London, she stayed close to me. Popsy was late, but arrived as if she was blown in by a strong wind.

'My darling!' she said, kissing Alessia. She was about forty-five years old and was wearing trousers and a shirt. 'Darling, you're so thin!'

'Popsy, this is Andrew,' said Alessia. 'He travelled with me. Can he come to lunch on Sunday?'

Popsy looked at me carefully. 'OK, darling. Anything you like.'

♦

I went to the Liberty Market office after leaving the airport. Tony Vine was there. He used to be a soldier, but now his work was the same as mine – getting kidnap victims back from their kidnappers.

'I thought you were in Colombia,' I said.

'Came back last week,' he said.

I used all of Saturday and some of Sunday morning to write my report about the Cenci kidnapping. Then I drove to Lambourn.

Popsy lived in a tall white house near the centre of the village. She was outside when I arrived.

'Alessia's round the back,' she said.

We walked behind the house and I saw a girl slowly riding a horse, and another girl watching her.

'Look at her,' said Popsy. 'She's supposed to be up on that horse, not watching my farm girl riding.'

Alessia turned round as we got closer. 'I was afraid you wouldn't come,' she said. She was wearing jeans and a shirt, and her face was still white. We went into the house and Popsy went off to the kitchen to cook some steaks. 'I shouldn't have come here,' Alessia said to me. 'I thought I would feel different, but I don't.'

'You will,' I said. I sat next to her, but not touching her. 'I'll help as much as I can, for as long as you want me to.'

♦

Popsy's steaks were excellent, but Alessia only ate half of hers.

'You must get strong again,' Popsy told her. 'You've worked hard to become a top jockey.'

'I telephoned Mike,' said Alessia. 'I told him I needed time.'

'Phone him again and tell him you can be ready to race in a week.'

'No! I can't –'

'My darling, you're a brave person. You can do it if you want to.'

'Who's Mike?' I asked.

'Mike Noland,' said Popsy. 'He's the trainer Alessia often rides for in England. He lives here in Lambourn.'

After the meal, Alessia and I went to look at some of the horses. 'I can't be ready in a week,' she told me. 'It's impossible.' She touched the nose of one of the animals. 'Do you ride?'

'No,' I said. 'And I've never been to the races.'

She looked shocked. 'Never? Would you like to go?'

'With you, yes. Very much.'

Her eyes filled with tears which she pushed away with her hand. 'That's always happening,' she said. 'Someone is kind, and I cry.'

'It's all right,' I said, and put my arm around her shoulders.

Chapter Seven

Three days later, Enrico Pucinelli telephoned me at the Liberty Market office. 'The youngest of the two kidnappers has been talking,' he said. 'He's told us the place Signorina Cenci went to, after the kidnap – a house in a quiet part of Bologna. We went there yesterday, and there's a room that's big enough for a tent. Has Signorina Cenci remembered any more?'

'Not yet,' I said.

On Thursday morning I went back to Lambourn to see Alessia, and arrived as some of Popsy's horses were going out for exercise. Popsy drove us up to the grass hills near Lambourn. It was a quiet place, except for the sound of a bird or two, and the sun was warm on our faces as we waited for the horses. They appeared in the distance, all ten of them. First as small shapes, then as riders and horses that seemed to be flying as they went past. We drove after them to the top of a hill, and found them walking in a circle. Alessia watched them closely.

'Tomorrow ...' She whispered the word but Popsy heard her.

'Today,' said Popsy, and she shouted at one of the riders. 'Bob! Come over here!'

Alessia looked at me, then followed three other horses down the hill.

The rider came across with his horse. He got off and Popsy helped Alessia on to the animal. Alessia looked at me, then followed three other horses down the hill.

'I thought she was never going to ride again,' said Popsy. She looked at me with her green eyes. 'Alessia told me about your job, and that you helped her father. She says she feels safe with you.' She paused. 'I didn't know there were people like you.'

'There are quite a few of us around the world.'

'What do you call yourself, if people ask?'

'Safety adviser, usually,' I said.

'It sounds very ordinary.'

'I want it to sound ordinary.'

We watched Alessia come back up the hill on the horse.

'Tomorrow?' Popsy asked her. 'With the other horses?'

Alessia smiled and nodded.

We went back to the house and she wrote a list of the

music she listened to after she was kidnapped. Music by Verdi.

'I did think of another thing,' she said. 'I dreamed it. I was walking out to a race, but I couldn't find my horse. I asked people, but they didn't know. And they were all catching trains, or something. Then someone said, "At least an hour to Viralto," and I woke up. I was hot, and I could hear my heart in my chest. I think it must be something I heard one of the kidnappers say.'

'Do you often go to Viralto?' I asked.

'No, I don't even know it.'

'I'll tell Pucinelli,' I said.

She came out to the car with me, and when I left she kissed me as if I'd known her for years.

Chapter Eight

'Viralto is a small village in the mountains,' Pucinelli told me over the phone. 'Are you sure she said Viralto?'

'Yes,' I said. 'Is it an hour's drive from Bologna?'

'I suppose so, if you know the way.'

'And does it have somewhere that makes bread?'

After a pause, he said, 'My men will go there immediately and search.'

'Say "Viralto" to the kidnapper who told you about the house,' I said.

'I will,' he said. 'He was one of the four men in masks who took Alessia. He says the name of your man in the picture is Giuseppe.'

'Enrico, you're a good detective. Before you go to Viralto, shall I ask Paolo Cenci to offer a reward for the return of any of the ransom money? And will you take the picture of Giuseppe with you?'

'Yes. I'll also take photographs of our two kidnappers, and of Alessia,' he said. 'Signor Cenci will surely agree to the reward.'

After we finished talking, I telephoned Cenci. He was very willing to offer the reward, so I phoned Pucinelli and told him.

The next day, Pucinelli phoned me again.

'The name of Viralto was a shock to the kidnapper who talks,' he told me. 'He says it means nothing to him, but he's lying. But we found nothing in Viralto. The village people were not talking. We went to the place that makes bread. The owner says he would know if Alessia came to the village, because he knows everything that happens there.'

'Do you believe him?'

'Yes, I'm afraid I do. We went to every house and we even asked some of the children, but we found nothing and we heard nothing. But I've looked at a map, and if you drive past Viralto the road goes up into the mountains. There's a place that used to be a castle but is now a hotel. Tomorrow, I'll go there.'

He phoned again late the next evening.

'Signorina Alessia was taken past Viralto and up to the hotel,' said Pucinelli. 'The hotel manager knows nothing, but we searched the small buildings around the hotel. In the past they were used by servants, or for farm animals and horses. Now they are for keeping meat and vegetables in, or for extra beds or blankets used in the hotel. But in one of them, in an upstairs room, we found a tent.'

'Congratulations!' I said, excitedly.

'The building is near the kitchens ... and they make their own bread.'

'Wonderful!'

'No, not wonderful. Nobody saw her there and nobody is saying anything. Vans deliver things to the hotel every day, and I think the signorina was taken to the hotel in one. Nobody would take special notice of another van "delivering" something to one of the small buildings.'

'Did you have any luck with the picture of the kidnapper?' I asked.

'No, nobody knows him. And nobody knows the two we have in prison.' He sounded tired. 'Perhaps one of the kidnappers stayed or worked at the Vistaclara in the past.'

'Vistaclara? Is that the name of the hotel?'

'Yes,' he said. 'In the past, there were horses there, but not enough people want to ride any more. They prefer to play tennis.'

'How long ago did they have horses?'

'More than five years,' he said. 'Before the manager came.'

Horses, I thought. Again.

Chapter Nine

During the first week in August, Pucinelli phoned several times. First to tell me the offer of a reward had been successful.

'A woman telephoned Cenci,' he said. 'She knows where part of the ransom money is hidden. Cenci says she sounds angry with somebody and is pleased that "he" will lose his money. But she won't say who "he" is. Tomorrow, we're going to the place she says the money can be found. If she's right, Cenci will send a reward to her. The address to send the reward is a small hotel. Perhaps we can find the woman and question her.'

The following evening, he phoned again. He sounded disappointed. 'We've found some of the money,' he said. 'But only fifty million lire.'

'Nearly twenty-five thousand pounds,' I said. 'Not the money of the chief kidnapper.'

'No,' he agreed. 'It was in a luggage **locker** at the railway station. The woman told Signor Cenci the number of the locker. We have left the money there, but we have changed the lock. If anyone tries to open it, he will have to ask for another key. Then we can catch him.'

'Phone me again when something happens,' I said.

Pucinelli telephoned two days later.

'The woman came for the reward and we followed her home. Her husband is a criminal. He likes other women and she gets very jealous. His name is Giovanni Santo, and the ticket for the luggage locker was in his wallet. He's now in prison and pouring out information like water from a tap. He's told us the names of all the kidnappers – there were seven. We already had two, and now we have Santo. At this minute, we have men out getting three others.'

'And Giuseppe?' I asked.

'Giuseppe is not one of them. He's the seventh, and he's the boss. Santo says he doesn't know his real name, or where he comes from or where he is now. And I believe him.'

Three nights later, he telephoned to say he had all six kidnappers in prison. 'And we've got back one hundred million lire of Cenci's money,' he said. 'But not Giuseppe.'

'You've done well, Enrico,' I told him.

'Thank you, my friend,' he said.

♦

Next day, I went to Lambourn. Alessia looked happier and there was colour in her cheeks at last.

'Hi,' she said. 'I've been shopping. That's the third time, and I've stopped feeling nervous. Almost.'

'Wonderful,' I said.

Her father had told her about the return of some of the ransom money. Now I told her that six of the kidnappers were in prison.

'The boss isn't one of them,' I said. 'The kidnappers know him as Giuseppe, but it's probably not his real name.'

She was quiet for a moment, then she said, 'I was thinking of going to the races next week. To Brighton, on Wednesday.'

'Can I come with you?' I asked.

She smiled. 'Yes, please.'

♦

We went to Brighton together, and everyone she met at the racecourse was pleased to see her.

'Alessia! How wonderful!'

'Alessia, how lovely to see you!'

I stayed near her, and she never moved a step without being certain I was following. Then, after the fourth race, I received a message to go to the Manager's office.

27

'I'll show you the way,' Alessia said. She looked worried. 'Perhaps it's bad news. I hope it's not Papa …'

We went quickly to the office and were met by the Course Manager.

He gave me a piece of paper. 'Can you please phone this number?' It was Liberty Market's telephone number.

'It's Andrew,' I said when the phone was answered.

'Thank God.' It was Gerry Clayton, one of the men at the office. 'A boy has disappeared from the beach at West Wittering. That's about an hour's drive from Brighton. Go and talk to the mother, will you?'

'Where is she?' I asked.

'The Breakwater Hotel, Beach Road. The father is staying next to his home telephone. Tony Vine is on his way to him now.' He read out the father's phone number. 'His name is John Nerrity. The child's name is Dominic, and the mother's name is Miranda. Mother and son were alone at the hotel, on holiday. Father is busy at home. Got all that?'

'Yes.'

'Get her to agree to calling the police, and call me later. Sorry about your day at the races.'

'I'll go now,' I said, and put down the phone.

I thanked the Course Manager and left his office. Alessia followed, looking worried.

'I have to go on a job – the kidnapping of a child,' I explained outside. 'I have to go to the child's mother. Can Mike Noland take you back to Lambourn?'

All her earlier fear seemed to come back into her face. 'Can't I come with you? I can help.'

I wasn't sure about that idea. I looked at my watch. 'Mrs Nerrity's waiting for me,' I said, trying to decide.

'Who?' Alessia said quickly.

'Nerrity. Miranda Nerrity. But …'

'I know her!' said Alessia. 'Or I've met her. Her husband is John Nerrity. Their horse won the Derby.'

I stared at her. *Horses again.* 'Let's go to the car,' I said. ' You can come if you want to, but we won't be back in Lambourn tonight.'

For an answer, she got into the passenger seat of the car. 'The Nerritys' horse won the Derby last year,' she said. 'It was called Ordinand. Don't you remember?' I didn't. 'That poor child.'

'His name's Dominic,' I said.

'How old is he?'

'I don't know.'

I drove fast through the golden summer afternoon, and came eventually to the Breakwater Hotel. It was next to the beach at West Wittering, and I stopped the car and pulled off my tie.

'Behave like a person on holiday,' I told Alessia. 'Walk into the hotel slowly. Smile, and talk to me. Don't look worried, OK?'

'You think ... somebody's watching?'

'Yes. Somebody usually makes sure the police don't arrive.'

I walked into the hotel with my arm around Alessia's shoulders. The girl behind the desk looked up.

'We think our friend, Mrs Nerrity, is staying here,' I said, smiling.

'And Dominic,' said Alessia.

'Can you phone through to their room?' I asked.

The girl did this and looked surprised to get an answer. I took the phone and spoke into it, still smiling.

'Miranda?' I said. 'This is Andrew Douglas. I'm downstairs.'

'Oh ... come up,' said a small voice.

A few moments later, Miranda Nerrity opened the door of her room. Her eyes were red and she was holding a wet handkerchief in one hand.

She found it hard to speak. 'The man in London said ... "you'll get Dominic back. Andrew Douglas will get him back ... he always does," he said. Oh my God! My baby ... please get him back for me!'

I took her to a chair. 'What happened? Tell us everything.'

She looked surprised to see Alessia, but she pointed at a piece of paper on the bed. 'A little girl gave it to me.'

'How old was the little girl?' I asked.

'What? Oh, about eight. I don't know.'

I read the words on the piece of paper:

WE HAVE YOUR BOY. PHONE YOUR HUSBAND AND TELL HIM TO GO HOME, WE'LL PHONE HIM THERE. TELL NO ONE. IF YOU WANT TO SEE YOUR BOY AGAIN, DON'T GO TO THE POLICE. IF YOU GET THE POLICE, WE'LL TIE A PLASTIC BAG OVER HIS HEAD. UNDERSTAND?

'How old is Dominic?' I asked.

'Three and a half,' said Miranda.

Chapter Ten

'We were on the beach and Dominic was making a castle,' explained Miranda. 'I was sitting not more than thirty metres away. I was watching him all the time, I really was.' Her voice was full of the terrible guilt she was feeling. 'It was the boat. There was a boat on the sand, and it was on fire. Everybody was watching it. Then I looked back ... and Dominic was gone. A little girl gave me the piece of paper ... and I read it. I ran up and down, shouting for him. And then I came up here ... I telephoned John.' She looked at me. 'He's so angry ... he blames me. I don't want to talk to him ... I can't ...'

'I need to speak to him,' I said, 'but I'll telephone from downstairs.' I left her with Alessia, then went downstairs and found a public telephone. Tony Vine answered from John Nerrity's number.

'The kidnappers have told him he'll get his son back safely if he pays five million pounds,' said Tony.

'My God!' I said. 'Has he got five million?'

'He's got a horse,' said Tony.

'Ordinand,' I said. 'The winner of the Derby.'

'That's right. The kidnappers want him to sell it. He's ... angry.'

'Mrs Nerrity is afraid of him,' I said.

'I'm not surprised,' said Tony.

I told him about the burning boat. 'It wasn't an accident, I'm sure.'

'Have you talked to the local police?'

'No, I have to get Miranda to say yes first. Have you?'

'No,' he said. 'I tell Mr Nerrity we can't help him without the local police, but he doesn't listen.'

We finished speaking, and I went down to the beach. The sea was coming in and the burned boat was almost in the water.

'Has anybody told the police?' I asked a man who was looking at it.

'I don't know,' he said. He didn't look very interested.

Two boys helped me pull the boat up the beach, so that the sea didn't take it away. Then I went back to the hotel and Miranda's room.

'We must get the police,' I told her.

'No, no!'

I nodded. 'It's the best thing to do. The kidnappers don't want to kill Dominic, they want to keep him safe and sell him back to you. They won't know if we tell the police.'

She looked confused. 'I don't know. John said ... keep quiet.'

I telephoned her husband's number again and spoke to Tony. 'Mrs Nerrity will let me phone the police, if her husband says yes.'

'I've told him we can't help unless we tell the police,' said Tony. 'He says OK. What was the boy wearing?'

I turned and asked Miranda.

'Red shorts,' she said. 'No shoes, no shirt. It was hot.'

I told Tony, then put down the phone.

Next, I drove Miranda and Alessia to Chichester. Nobody followed us, I was sure. But I parked the car and walked to the police station alone.

♦

Detective Superintendent Eagler was a thin little man. His suit was old and hung loosely on his body. He didn't look like a detective, but he listened to my story and looked at the message on the piece of paper.

'Will you talk to Mrs Nerrity in my car?' I asked him. 'I don't think it's wise for her to come into a police station.'

He agreed with me, and I went back to the car. We met him some minutes later, in another road. He got into the passenger seat without saying anything, and I drove out into the countryside. Miranda told her story to the detective, with tears running down her face and her whole body shaking. When she finished speaking, Eagler put a hand on her arm.

'We all have to be calm, Mrs Nerrity,' he said. 'You've had a terrible shock, but we must think of the boy now.' He looked at Alessia.

'Alessia was kidnapped,' I explained, then told him about the kidnapping in Italy. I told him about the horses.

'You think the same person is responsible for both kidnappings?'

I nodded. 'And there was another kidnapping in Italy, before Alessia's. The family sold a racehorse to pay the ransom.' I looked at Alessia. 'The chief kidnapper is somebody who knows the racing world. He knew your father was much richer than the father of other jockeys.'

She nodded, slowly understanding. 'And he knew the owner of Ordinand had a son,' she said.

Miranda had stopped crying. Eagler and I got out of the car and walked a few metres away. He knew about Liberty Market and seemed happy for me to help. 'What more can you tell me?' he asked.

'The man who kidnapped Alessia used local men to help him,' I said. 'All six are in prison now, but their boss has disappeared. He used the name Giuseppe. I'll get you our picture of him, and a report of the kidnapping.'

Chapter Eleven

John and Miranda Nerrity lived in a large, expensive house just outside London. When we arrived that evening, Tony Vine was with Nerrity and another man.

'This is Detective Superintendent Rightsworth,' said Tony.

The detective gave me a cool look and said nothing. Alessia and Miranda came into the room behind me. I watched John Nerrity's angry face as he looked at his wife. He gave her no kiss, and didn't touch her.

'Do you realize I can't sell Ordinand because someone is already selling him for me?' he said to her coldly. 'I've borrowed money for the business, and the money for Ordinand is to pay that back. Can't you do *anything*? Can't you even look after a child?'

Miranda made a small crying sound and Alessia and I helped her across to a sofa. Rightsworth went to ask her some questions, and her husband followed him. Tony and I went over to a window to talk quietly.

'Have you heard from the kidnappers again?' I asked.

'No,' Tony answered.

I looked at Rightsworth. 'I don't think he likes us.'

'He doesn't,' said Tony.

'And Nerrity has no money,' I said.

'His business is in trouble.' Tony looked over at Miranda who was crying again. 'She was his secretary before they were married.'

The telephone rang suddenly, and everyone jumped. Nerrity walked over to it, and Tony switched on a machine for us to listen to the call.

'Is that John Nerrity?' a loud voice said. It was a man's voice.

'Yes,' Nerrity said, not breathing.

'You'll find a cassette in a box by your front gate. Listen to it, and do everything it tells you to do.' Then the phone went silent.

Nerrity hurried towards the front door.

I spoke quietly to Alessia. 'Take Miranda into the kitchen for some food or a drink. I don't want her to hear the cassette.'

She nodded, then went across and suggested a cup of tea to the frightened woman. Miranda agreed, and they went out of the room.

Nerrity came back with a brown box, and Rightsworth put on a pair of plastic gloves and carefully used a knife to open it. The cassette was inside. Nerrity pointed to an expensive cassette machine on a wall and the policeman put the cassette in it.

The voice filled the room …

'Listen, Nerrity. We took your boy. If you want him back in one piece, do what we tell you. If you don't, we'll take a knife and cut him. We'll cut off his finger … or other parts of his body … and send them to you. Understand, Nerrity?

'You've got a horse. Sell it. You ought to get six million. We want five million, and we want it in seven days. And keep away from the police or we'll kill the boy. You won't even get his body back. OK, Nerrity? That's the message.'

The voice stopped, and it was a shocked and silent minute before anyone moved, then Rightsworth took the cassette and the brown box.

'I'm going now, and I'm taking these with me,' he told Nerrity.

'*Please* be careful,' said Nerrity. 'If they know the police …'

'We'll be careful,' said Rightsworth.

Nerrity became calmer. 'I'm not paying that ransom, I can't. I borrowed money for my business, and the money for Ordinand is going to save me. I'm not going to lose everything for those kidnappers.'

Now it was clear. He didn't love his son enough to lose everything for him.

'I think we may get your son back for less than half a million,' said Tony, coldly. 'We'll begin by offering a hundred thousand.'

'I – I do like the boy,' said Nerrity. 'I don't see him very often. I work, I go to the races, I go out with business friends. But it was Miranda who suggested we have a child. And now …'

I'd heard enough. I put Alessia in the car then talked to Tony quietly in the garden. 'Take Giuseppe's picture and the Cenci

The voice stopped, and it was a shocked and silent minute before anyone moved.

kidnapping report to Eagler. We'll meet at the Breakwater Hotel in Wittering in the morning. We'll go to the beach and ask some questions.'

Then I took Alessia back to Lambourn.

◆

Tony was already on the beach when I got to West Wittering the next morning.

'Eagler had the same idea,' he said. 'He has some of his men and women dressed like people on holiday. They're here on the beach, quietly asking questions.'

'Have you seen Eagler?'

'Yes,' said Tony. 'He says the burned boat was stolen.'

Children were making a castle in the wet sand and we watched them.

'A little girl of about eight gave Miranda the piece of paper,' I said. 'She's probably here again today.'

Instead of answering, Tony walked across to a man and woman who were playing with a ball. He spoke a few words to them, then came back.

'They'll look for her,' he said, and then I knew the two were police officers. 'They've talked to people who saw the boat and they have a picture of Giuseppe, but nobody has recognized him.'

We met Eagler later that afternoon, in a café in Itchenor, a few miles away. He gave us some news about the small girl.

'A policewoman found her,' he said. 'You were right, she was on the beach again today. She's seven years old, but she can't describe the man who gave her the piece of paper. She says he gave her some sweets, and she's afraid to tell her mother.'

'Kidnappers don't usually take their victims very far,' said Tony. 'And lots of people **rent** houses for holidays around here.'

'Thousands of people,' agreed Eagler.

'Perhaps one house was rented last week,' I suggested.

He nodded. 'We'll ask some questions. The boy may have been taken away in a boat. A woman told us there was a motorboat near the beach before the other boat was burned, and a man was standing in the water next to it.'

'What did he look like?' I asked.

'Just a man,' said Eagler. 'The woman was more interested in the boat.'

'Tell me if you find a house that's likely to be the one,' Tony told him. 'I'll look at it and find out if the boy's there. If he is, I'll get him out.'

Chapter Twelve

There was a message for me at the Breakwater Hotel, to telephone Alessia as soon as possible. I did this, and heard her worried voice.

'Andrew, Miranda is frightened.'

'What's happened?' I said.

'John Nerrity is going to pretend to obey the kidnappers. He's going to pretend to get the money. And when the money is handed over to the kidnappers, Superintendent Rightsworth and his men are going to jump out and catch the kidnappers. They're going to make them tell the police the place where Dominic is hidden.' Her voice was high and frightened. 'The police did that in Bologna with me, didn't they?'

'Yes,' I said. 'It's the wrong thing to do. It's too dangerous.'

'Superintendent Rightsworth is telling John he doesn't have to pay the ransom money. And John is going to tell Liberty Market he doesn't want their help any more. He says it's a waste of money ...'

'We'll try to make him change his mind,' I said.

I finished speaking to Alessia and told Tony about Nerrity's plans.

'He's a fool,' said Tony. 'We must find the kid first, mustn't we?'

♦

Next day, Eagler gave me a list of houses. 'The houses on this list were for rent two weeks ago,' he said. 'Now there are people in them. The first eleven are all near the water, and were rented only a day or two before the people moved in.'

'We'll look at them,' I said.

'I've some good men who could help.'

'No, thanks,' I said. 'I'd prefer Tony to do it.'

Later, I showed Tony the list.

'I'll look at some of them tonight,' he said. 'Then I'll sleep tomorrow, and look at some more tomorrow night.'

He came back at daylight.

'Nine of the eleven houses have holiday people in them,' he told me. 'I went into four to be completely certain.'

I imagined him silently walking around the houses as the

Tony turned on the radio receiver again ... and this time we heard the voice.

people slept. If he wasn't so honest, I thought, he would make a good burglar.

'I'm not sure about the other two,' he said. 'One had a **burglar alarm**, so I didn't go in. But I left some **listening devices** on the walls, so we can go back and listen. The other had three floors and was difficult to get into. I left listening devices there, too.'

He had a shower, and by 8.30 we were driving to Itchenor. Tony was listening to a radio receiver in the car.

'We're getting near the house with the burglar alarm,' he told me, but nothing came from the radio receiver. 'They're not awake yet. We'll go on to the other place.'

We went further north before stopping again. Tony turned on the radio receiver again ... and this time we heard the voice.

'Give him his breakfast and shut him up if he starts crying.'

It was the voice we had heard on the cassette at Nerrity's house.

'My God!' I said, not believing it.

A different voice, said, *'I don't like this job'*. There were no more sounds for some minutes and we sat and waited. Then the second voice spoke again, but from further away, on the top floor. *'Here you are, boy. Eat this.'* There was no answer. *'Eat it!'* the voice said, angrily. He came downstairs again and we heard him speak to the first man. *'How soon can we get rid of him?'*

'Be patient,' said the first man. *'Nerrity has to sell his horse. We told him a week.'*

'We ask for five to frighten the father, but we take half a million. Peter's done this before, so listen to him and we'll all be rich.'

We had heard enough.

'We won't tell Eagler ... yet,' I said. 'But tonight ...'

Tony smiled. 'Tonight,' he said.

Chapter Thirteen

The day passed slowly. At five o'clock in the afternoon, I phoned Eagler and told him Tony had found the kidnappers.

'I don't believe it!' he said. 'Where are they?'

'Waiting and watching to see if the police do anything,' I said. 'If you arrive too soon, they'll kill the boy. Get your men to Chichester police station by one o'clock in the morning.'

'Where do my men go?' asked Eagler.

'I'll tell you after one o'clock.'

He didn't like that, but he had to agree to it because I wasn't going to tell him any more. A long time after it was dark, I went to meet Tony. He'd been near the house all day, listening to the men.

'It's quiet in there now,' he said. 'There's another man called Kevin with them. They also had a phone call from Peter. I only heard their part of the conversation, but he was the one who took the boy.'

'I'm phoning Eagler after one o'clock,' I said, and I told Tony my plans for the policemen.

'You're not taking any chances,' he said, smiling.

'No mistakes,' I said. 'Not this time.'

Some time after one o'clock, I spoke to Eagler on the phone. I told him when to move his men, and where to take them.

'Tell them to be completely silent,' I said. 'We'll come to meet you. It may be a long time after you get there, but wait.'

'Is that all you're going to tell me?' he said.

'We'll tell you the rest when we meet you.' I put down the phone.

Tony drove us to Itchenor and parked in a row of cars round the corner from the kidnappers' house. He took some make-up from his pocket, and used it to blacken his hands and face. I turned on the radio receiver to check sounds inside the house. Everything was silent.

Tony gave me the make-up. 'Blacken your face,' he said.

It was 2.15 a.m. We got out of the car into the quiet street. I took a soft bag from the back of the car and then we walked to the corner of the street. Tony disappeared into the shadows and I waited, counting up to ten. Then, keeping close to the ground, I went across to the wall on the right-hand side of the kidnappers' house.

Tony was climbing that wall. I could see his dark shape. I waited, listening to the sound of my heart. After a long time, something hit me gently in the face. I put my hand up to catch it and put my fingers around the **rope**. I tied the soft bag to the rope, then pulled it twice. The rope and bag disappeared into the darkness above me.

I waited. Suddenly, the bag was down with me again. It was heavy now, not empty. I took it into my arms and pulled the rope again. It dropped down in the shadows around my feet and I picked it up. I didn't hear Tony come down, but he was standing next to me a few moments later. We ran quickly and quietly to the car.

*Tony was climbing that wall. I could see his dark shape. I waited,
listening to the sound of my heart.*

I took the bag into the back seat ... and took out one very
small boy.

He was sleeping heavily, and I put a blanket around him to
keep him warm while Tony drove to the place I had told Eagler
to take his men. It was the other house on the list – the one with
the burglar alarm.

Eagler came to the car.

'Dominic is here,' I said. 'We're taking him to his mother. We
got the boy, you can get the kidnappers. And we don't want
Liberty Market's name in the newspapers. We're only useful to
people if we're not known.'

He didn't argue. 'All right. Where do we go?'

Tony told him. 'The boy was on the top floor,' he said. 'The
men are on the floor below. Three of them.'

'The chief kidnapper was supposed to be coming tomorrow

or the day after,' I said. 'I don't think he will now. But he might telephone.'

Tony started the car and we drove away. Dominic slept with his head against my shoulder, and he woke up near the end of the journey.

'Hello, Dominic,' I said. 'We're taking you home.' He watched my face without speaking. 'You're safe now. Nobody can hurt you.'

He was still wearing his red shorts. The kidnappers had given him a shirt that was too big, but no socks or shoes. But the blanket was keeping him warm.

The Nerrity house was dark when we arrived. It was 4 a.m. Tony stopped the car outside, and a light went on upstairs when we knocked on the door. After several minutes, John Nerrity opened the door.

'Who is it? What do you want?' he said.

Tony stepped into the light coming from the door. 'Tony Vine.'

'Go away,' Nerrity was angry. 'I don't want Liberty Market –'

'We have your kid,' said Tony, coldly. 'Tell Mrs Nerrity.'

The door opened and she was behind him. I got out of the car, carrying Dominic.

'Here he is,' I said. 'He's safe.'

Her arms opened and she took him, unable to say a word.

Chapter Fourteen

Eagler took the three kidnappers without a fight. 'They aren't talking,' he said over the phone later. 'But they will.'

Alessia also telephoned. 'Miranda phoned. She told me you brought Dominic home. She can't speak for tears, but this time they're mostly happy. I suggested she and Dominic came to Lambourn tomorrow. Popsy suggests you come too ... and I think it would be wonderful if you could.'

42

So next morning, I drove to Lambourn. Alessia came out of the house to meet me. She looked happy – really happy – for the first time since her own kidnap. Dominic was in the house with Miranda and Popsy.

'Hello, Dominic,' I said. He stared at me with big blue eyes.

We had lunch in the kitchen. Miranda ate little, and Dominic ate nothing. Afterwards, Popsy drove us up into the Lambourn hills and we sat on the grass. It was wonderfully peaceful. Later, Alessia, Popsy and I went for a short walk.

'It's time I went back to racing,' Alessia said suddenly.

'My darling!' said Popsy, excitedly. 'Do you mean it?'

'I think I do,' said Alessia, smiling nervously.

I put my arms around her and kissed her. It began as a kiss of congratulation ... but it ended as something quite different.

'Did ... did you mean that?' Alessia wanted to know.

'It was ... a surprise,' I said.

She stared at me for a moment. 'It certainly was.'

Popsy was amused. We walked back and found Miranda lying on the grass, almost asleep. Dominic was lying with her, with his eyes closed. Miranda woke up, but Dominic was still asleep when we drove away. Miranda was holding him close to her in the back seat.

We were almost back at the house when I saw her bend over him to listen. Alessia looked at me, then did the same.

'Stop the car,' she told Popsy suddenly, and Popsy obeyed.

A small sound was coming from Dominic. Music.

'He knows it!' said Alessia, excitedly. 'That music is from *Il Trovatore*. Verdi. I heard it five times a day for six weeks.'

'My God!' I said. 'Drive home, Popsy.'

When we got back to the house, I went to my car and got out a picture of Guiseppe. I put it on the kitchen table, in front of Dominic. He looked at it calmly for a moment, then he turned back to his mother.

I was disappointed.

'*Ciao, bambino*,' said Dominic.

Alessia and I stared at him.

'What did you say?' Alessia asked him.

He didn't answer.

'He said " *Ciao, bambino* ",' I said. 'Does he know any Italian?'

'No, of course not,' said Miranda.

'Goodbye, baby,' said Popsy. 'Didn't he say that?'

I showed him the picture of Giuseppe again. 'What was the man's name, Dominic? Was it … Michael?'

Dominic said nothing.

'Was it David?'

Dominic shook his head.

'Was his name Peter?'

Dominic was still for a long time. Then, very slowly, he nodded.

'*Ciao, bambino*,' he said again.

◆

I told Eagler.

'We'll put that picture all over England,' he said.

'Show it to racing people,' I said. 'He knows the racing world. Somebody, somewhere, might know him.'

'Our three kidnappers haven't been saying anything,' he said. 'But they will now.'

During the next two weeks, I went to see Alessia race. She didn't win the first few races, but Mike Noland wasn't worried.

'You'll do better next time,' he said each time.

And he was right. At the end of the second week, she won two races.

I watched her smiling and saw the excitement in her eyes. At first she seemed to want me to be there waiting for her, but slowly she became more confident and happy. She began to think of the future.

'I'm going home,' she said one day. 'To Italy. To see Papa.'

'I'll miss you,' I said.

'Will you?' She smiled at me. 'I have so much to thank you for. But I'll be back to race here next summer.'

Next summer seemed a long time away.

'Don't forget me,' she said.

'No,' I said.

She went to Italy and my days seemed empty.

News of the Nerrity kidnapping caused the Jockey Club★ to become nervous and I went to see the President, Morgan Freemantle.

'There have been three kidnappings in the racing world,' I said. 'A racehorse owner in Italy, Alessia Cenci, and John Nerrity's son.'

'You think the same person is responsible for all three?' he said.

'Yes,' I said. 'We don't know if he'll try again, but others may copy his idea. They may use kidnapping to make somebody sell a valuable horse, and then take the money.'

'The Jockey Club will give you whatever help we can,' he said.

'Thank you,' I said, surprised.

I telephoned the Villa Francese one evening and spoke to Alessia.

'How are you?' I asked.

'I'm very well,' she said. 'Really, I am. I've ridden in several races since I came back, and I've won two. Do you remember Brunelleschi?'

'The horse you didn't ride in the Derby.'

'That's right. He was one of my winners last week, and they're sending him to Washington to run in the International race at Laurel racecourse. They've asked me to ride him.'

'Washington DC? America? Are you going?'

'I ... don't know. What do you think?'

'Go if you can,' I said.

'Can you come with me?' she asked.

'No, I'm sorry,' I said. 'I've work to do here.'

★ *The Jockey Club.* The people who control horse racing in England.

45

But something happened that changed things.

Morgan Freemantle was invited to Laurel for a week. He was the special guest of the racecourse president. On the second day of his visit, he was kidnapped.

PART THREE: WASHINGTON DC

Chapter Fifteen

The Jockey Club received the kidnappers' telephone call at two o'clock in the afternoon. They wanted ten million pounds or Morgan Freemantle would be killed. There would be another message later.

The woman who took the call thought it was a joke. Then she phoned Mr Freemantle's hotel in Washington and discovered he wasn't there. More phone calls. Morgan Freemantle had disappeared.

The Jockey Club asked Liberty Market to help, and I got on a plane to Washington the next morning.

Laurel racecourse was an hour's drive from the city. I asked to see Mr Rickenbacker, the president. He was a big man with white hair, and Liberty Market had told him I was coming. He shook my hand.

'What a mess!' he said. 'One day Morgan is telling me about the Nerrity kidnapping, and the next day *he's* kidnapped!'

'What happened?' I asked.

'Morgan was staying at the Ritz Carlton hotel,' said Rickenbacker. 'We have cars and drivers who pick up guests and bring them to the racecourse. A driver went to the Ritz Carlton, but it wasn't one of our drivers. He asked for Mr Freemantle and Morgan came down, left his key at the desk, and went with the driver. That's all anyone knows.'

'What was the driver like?'

'The man at the hotel desk can't remember. He only remembers that the man didn't speak like an American. Another driver arrived, and was told Morgan had already gone. The driver wasn't surprised. Mistakes happen, and he thought it was just another mistake. Nobody was worried until I received the telephone call from the Jockey Club in England.'

'Have you told the police?'

'Sure,' he said. 'The police in Washington are working on it. The man controlling things is Captain Kent Wagner. He knows you're coming.'

'OK,' I said. 'Thanks.'

'All the owners, trainers and jockeys from other countries are coming to a special breakfast in the club tomorrow morning,' he said. 'They'll meet with people from the newspapers and television. Why don't you come?'

'I'll come if I can.' I asked if I could use his phone, then telephoned Liberty Market in London. Gerry Clayton answered.

'Any news from the Jockey Club?' I asked.

'Yes, they got a cassette in the post. Do you want to hear it?'

There was a short pause, then an American voice spoke.

'If you people at the Jockey Club want Morgan Freemantle back, it's going to cost you ten million English pounds. You have one week to get the money, then we'll tell you the next thing to do. Freemantle wants to talk to you. Listen.'

There was another pause, then Fremantle's voice. He sounded calm. *'If you don't pay the ransom money, they'll kill me. That's what they tell me, and I believe it.'* The cassette stopped suddenly.

'Did you hear all that?' asked Gerry Clayton.

'Yes,' I said.

◆

Captain of Detectives, Kent Wagner was in his office. He was a big man with a soft voice, and he stared at me with a cool look in his eye.

47

'Kidnappers never win in the United States,' he said. 'Now, what can you tell me?'

'Quite a lot,' I said. 'We think this is the third, or perhaps the fourth kidnapping by the same person.' I told him what had happened in Italy and in England. I played him the cassettes from the kidnappers, and he listened to the cassette in London over the phone. Then I gave him a copy of my picture of Giuseppe-Peter.

'We'll put copies of this all over the city,' he said. 'If the Nerrity child recognized him, anybody can.' He looked at me closely. 'Does this man Giuseppe-Peter frighten you?'

'Yes, he does,' I said. 'He's calm, he's clever, and he's prepared to kill.'

Kent Wagner looked at his hands. 'And he may not like *you*, Andrew.'

I was surprised when he used my first name. 'I don't think he knows I'm alive, Kent,' I replied.

Chapter Sixteen

I went to the breakfast at the racecourse the next morning, hoping to see Alessia. The race-club rooms were crowded with sports-writers and television reporters.

'Orange juice?' somebody said, handing me a glass.

The crowd began moving into a large side room. There were long tables ready for the breakfast, and I was trying to decide whether or not to stay when I heard a surprised voice by my left ear say, 'Andrew?' I turned. And there she was.

I hadn't seen her for six weeks. Before, she had been the victim of a kidnapping and part of my job, someone just passing through my life. But now I felt the sudden excitement growing inside me as I looked at her. I put my arms tightly around her, and she did the same to me.

'Well ...' I looked into her brown eyes. 'Want a lover?'

She stopped breathing for a second, laughed a little, but didn't answer the question. 'We're over there,' she said, pointing across the room. 'Do join us.'

Paolo Cenci welcomed me by putting his arms around me. 'This is the man who brought Alessia back safely,' he said in Italian to the three other people at the table. He smiled at me. 'Meet Bruno and Beatrice Goldoni,' he said in English. 'They are the owners of Brunelleschi.'

I shook hands with a man of about sixty and a woman a few years younger. They nodded pleasantly but didn't speak.

'And Silvio Lucchese, Brunelleschi's trainer,' Paolo Cenci said, introducing the last of the three; a dark, thin little man.

I said very little during breakfast. The others talked in Italian, about Brunelleschi and the race. I thought about my feelings for Alessia, and the question she hadn't answered. Afterwards, there were short interviews with trainers, jockeys and many of the owners.

'What was it like being kidnapped?' one reporter asked Alessia.

'Horrible,' she said. 'I feel very sorry for Morgan Freemantle.'

She sat down and turned to me. 'When I heard about Morgan Freemantle, I thought about Liberty Market. That's why you're here, isn't it? Will you find him, like Dominic?'

'I don't know.'

A little later I said goodbye to the others, and Alessia walked out of the dining-room with me. I put my arm around her.

'Not here,' she said.

I let my arm fall away. 'I'm staying at the Sherryatt.'

'I'm at the Regency,' she said.

'Can I take you to dinner?'

'I can't,' she said. 'But we could go for a drive this afternoon.'

◆

For the first hour of our drive, we had to listen to Beatrice Goldoni. She was visiting the hotel's hairdresser and Paolo Cenci suggested we took her with us to Washington. It was difficult to say no.

She seemed happy and excited as we drove into the city. But when we left her at the Regency, the excitement seemed to be mixed with guilt.

'Perhaps she's meeting a lover,' joked Alessia as we drove away.

'Is it OK if we just drive around?' I said.

She watched me. 'You're looking for Morgan Freemantle, aren't you?'

'For possible hiding places, yes. Private houses, probably north or west of the centre of the city, because the Ritz Carlton is there.'

There were miles of streets in which he could be hidden. Kent Wagner was looking for recently rented houses, but there must be hundreds of them. I realized his job was impossible.

'We've done enough,' I said at 3.30. 'Are you hungry?'

We went back to my room at the Sherryatt hotel and ordered salads and a bottle of wine. The food arrived and we ate it, then we looked silently at each other. Alessia pushed her plate away and stared thoughtfully into her wine glass.

'Since the kidnap … I've thought of kissing, of love … but I can't. I went out with someone two or three times. He wanted to kiss me … his mouth felt like rubber to me.' She looked at me. 'I know the way I *should* feel … and I don't.'

I walked over to the window. 'I do love you,' I said in a voice that sounded strange.

'Andrew!' She came towards me.

I tried to smile, to make my voice light. 'There's always time. You ride races now, and you go shopping. It all took time.' I put my arms around her and kissed her lightly on her cheek. 'Let me know when rubber begins feeling like lips.'

She put her head on my shoulder and we held each other.

♦

She rode her big race the next day, and I watched from high above in the president's dining-room. I watched Brunelleschi push through the other horses into fourth place. I saw them come round the top bend, all close together. I saw Alessia moving

I saw Alessia moving Brunelleschi away from the others, and going fast towards the last corner and the finish.

Brunelleschi away from the others, and going fast towards the last corner and the finish. Two of the horses in front seemed to be slowing down, but Brunelleschi ran on.

She won the race. I saw her being photographed and interviewed afterwards. I saw her laughing and saw the excitement on her face.

I was delighted. And I was lonely.

When I got back to my hotel, there was a message for me. Liberty Market had called. I phoned and spoke to Gerry Clayton.

'Your friend Pucinelli phoned from Bologna,' he said. 'I couldn't understand him very well, but I think he's found Giuseppe-Peter.'

Chapter Seventeen

It was eight o'clock the following morning when I finally spoke to Pucinelli. He had been in Milan.

'Where are you?' he said over the phone. 'Your office said America.'

'Yes, Washington,' I said. 'Have you really found Giuseppe-Peter?'

'Yes and no,' said Pucinelli. 'He lives near Milan and he's thirty-four. He went to Milan University, and a student friend who recognized his picture told us about him. He left university without taking his final examinations. They made him leave because he stole some money.'

'Did he!' I said.

'We also have information from some racing people. They say he's not well known in the horse world, and he never goes to the races. He no longer sees his family and his father doesn't speak to him any more, because of the bad things he's done.'

'The horse world told you this?' I said.

'Yes, somebody recognized him.'

'What's his name?' I asked.

'His father owns the racehorse, Brunelleschi,' he said. 'Giuseppe-Peter's real name is Pietro Goldoni.'

Washington DC seemed to stand still. I stopped breathing.

'Are you there, Andrew?' said Pucinelli.

I let out a long breath. 'Have you heard about Morgan Freemantle?'

'Who? I've been busy in Milan. Who is Morgan Freemantle?'

I told him. I also said, 'Bruno and Beatrice Goldoni are in Washington. I've talked to them. Brunelleschi won the International race yesterday afternoon. Alessia Cenci rode it.'

He was silent. Then he said, 'Pietro Goldoni is in Washington.'

'Yes,' I said.

'You knew that.'

'I was sure Giuseppe-Peter was here, yes,' I said. 'You've done well, Enrico. I congratulate you.'

After I had finished speaking to him, I phoned Kent Wagner and explained. 'The Goldonis are going to New York today,' I said after I had told him everything. 'Mrs Goldoni told me. They've been staying here at the Regency.'

'Are you still at the Sherryatt?' he asked.

'Yes.'

'Stay by the phone.'

I put down the phone and there was a knock at the door. It was a woman waiting to clean the room.

'How long will you be?' I asked.

'Twenty minutes,' she said.

Downstairs, I told the girl behind the desk that I was going to be in the bar. 'Please tell me if there are any phone calls for me,' I said.

I sat and thought about Beatrice Goldoni, and about the guilty look on her face the afternoon before. It wasn't a lover Beatrice was going to meet, it was her son. A son she still loved, even if her husband did not speak to him. Pietro probably arranged the meeting and I was certain she didn't know he was a kidnapper. She couldn't keep a secret like that. But how much had Paolo Cenci told her? Did she know about Dominic?

Beatrice talked a lot. She talked all the way to Washington in the car. Did she go on talking to her son, afterwards? *Remember Alessia, who was kidnapped? There's a young man with her. He's the one who helped her get back safely. Paolo Cenci told us he helped a little boy, Dominic, in England ...* Talk, talk, talk.

I went back to the desk to tell them I was leaving, and I asked them to prepare my bill. Then I phoned Wagner again.

'Come down here,' he said. 'I'll find a place for you to stay so that Goldoni will never find you.'

I went to my room to get my things. I unlocked my door and went in.

There were three men in there, and they were wearing work clothes with the words International Carpet company on the front and back of them. The furniture was pushed against the walls, and they were putting down a large carpet in the centre.

'What …?' I began. Then I thought: it's Sunday.

I turned round ready to run, but I was too late. A fourth man was closing the door. He walked towards me, his arms reaching for me. I looked into his eyes … and I knew him. Everything happened very fast. Something went over my head. I was pushed to the floor, and I felt a sharp pain in my leg. 'They're putting me inside the carpet,' I thought.

It was the last thought I had for a long time.

I woke up feeling cold. I was sitting on the ground against a tree, and my hands were the other side of the tree, behind my back. They were held by a rope.

And I had no clothes on. *Kidnapped*, I thought. *Me!*

I looked around. Only more trees. It was quiet, but I could hear the sound of traffic, so I was near the city. I could stand up, and I could walk sideways around the tree. I opened my mouth and shouted, 'Help!' I shouted it many times, but nothing happened.

Time went by. Occasionally, aeroplanes flew above me, and then it began to rain. Later on, it got dark. I was going to be there all night, I thought. Well, OK, I was strong and healthy. I tried not to think about the cold, tried not to think about hot food. I slept for an hour or two, then just waited for daylight to come. Did he intend to leave me there to die? I wondered. And where's the Verdi? I wouldn't mind some Verdi.

Daylight came. A grey day with low clouds in the sky. I didn't hear him coming, but he was suddenly there, wearing a brown leather jacket.

'Your name is Andrew Douglas,' he said in English.

I looked at him but didn't reply.

'You will speak on a cassette for me,' he said.

'All right.'

I was pushed to the floor, and I felt a sharp pain in my leg. 'They're putting me inside the carpet,' I thought.

He looked surprised. 'You do not ask … who I am?'

'You're one of the men who kidnapped me from the hotel,' I said.

'What is my name?'

'I don't know,' I said.

'It is Peter.'

He went away and was gone for about an hour. When he came back, he was carrying a bag. He gave me a piece of paper.

'You will say those words,' he said.

I read the message. It said:

I AM ANDREW DOUGLAS. JOCKEY CLUB, GET TEN MILLION POUNDS. SEND A SPECIAL BANKER'S CHEQUE TO ACCOUNT NUMBER ZL327/42806, CREDIT HELVETIA, ZURICH, SWITZERLAND. AFTER THAT, WAIT. THE POLICE MUST STAY AWAY. WHEN ALL IS OK, I WILL BE FREE. IF THE MONEY CANNOT BE TAKEN OUT OF THE SWISS BANK, I WILL BE KILLED.

'They won't pay ten million,' I said. 'They might pay one hundred thousand pounds.'

'That is stupid.'

'Perhaps fifty thousand more.'

We looked at each other silently. 'Five million,' he said.

'The Jockey Club has no money,' I said. 'They aren't rich people.'

'They have five million,' he said. 'I know.'

'Two hundred thousand, no more,' I said.

He walked away into the trees, and I guessed he wanted to think without me watching him. He came back eventually.

'You will say the words I wish you to say. If I do not like it, we will start again.' He took a cassette machine from his bag and switched it on, then held the piece of paper for me to read it.

'This is Andrew Douglas,' I said. 'The ransom for Morgan Freemantle is now five million pounds – '

He switched off the machine. 'I did not tell you to say that.'

'No, but it will save time.'

He thought about this for a moment, told me to start again, and switched the machine on.

'This is Andrew Douglas,' I said. 'The ransom for Morgan Freemantle is now five million pounds. Send a special banker's cheque to account number ZL327/42806, Credit Helvetia, Zurich, Switzerland. Morgan Freemantle will then be returned. Do not inform the police. After the money is moved from the account, I will be free.'

I stopped speaking. He switched off the machine and said, 'You have not finished. Say: unless these things happen, you will be killed.' He switched on the machine again.

'If these things don't happen,' I said, 'I'll be killed.'

Whatever happens, I thought, he will kill me. He put the cassette machine into his bag, then began to take out something. Fear rushed through me, but it wasn't a gun or a knife, it was a bottle.

'Soup,' he said. And he put the bottle to my mouth.

It was chicken soup – cold and thick – and I drank all of it. He watched without speaking, then put the bottle back in the bag. After that, he went away.

Chapter Eighteen

The rain came again. It rained for hours and the night was long and cold, but my skin dried when the rain stopped. As daylight came, I sat wondering if he was going to come back.

He did. Wearing the same jacket, carrying the same bag. There was another bottle of soup – warm this time – and it tasted like beef.

'I understand it was you who found the boy, in England,' he said. I said nothing. He put his hand into the bag and took out a copy of the picture of his face. 'You did this. I had to leave Italy because of this. In England, again this picture. This picture is here, in America, isn't it?' I didn't answer. 'Soon I will look different. When I have the ransom money, I will disappear.'

'The Jockey Club won't pay five million,' I said. 'The club members will argue, they'll take weeks deciding who should pay the most. Every day that you wait, the police will be getting closer to you.'

After a pause, he said, 'There are about one hundred members. They can pay thirty thousand pounds each. That is three million. Tomorrow you will make another message. You will tell them they must pay three million, or Freemantle will die and you will die.'

He turned and walked away.

It began raining again. I was tired of that place. I hated the rain, the rope, the cold wet ground. I was angry and I began to kick and shake the tree.

It moved.

I knocked my back against it, and something moved under my feet in the soft, wet ground. I began to dig with my toes, then went round the tree and sat down and dug with my fingers. I uncovered something hard.

A tree **root**.

I thought. Let this wonderful rain pour down and make the ground softer, wetter! It's my only chance.

♦

Hour after hour it rained, and I went on digging. Now I could push the tree backwards and forwards. Some of the roots came out of the ground easily, others took longer. Suddenly, the whole tree was falling and I was falling with it, down on to the wet brown leaves.

I had to dig up each root before I could get my arms under them, but at last I was free. It took only a few more minutes to push my body through my tied-up arms, one leg after the other, and finish with my hands in front of me. It was still raining, and beginning to get dark.

I remembered the direction Giuseppe-Peter came from, and I

walked the opposite way, through the trees. After several minutes I saw some lights, then some houses.

I forgot I had no clothes on and was walking towards one of the houses when I heard a car. I was standing in the brilliant lights from the car as it turned towards the house. It stopped suddenly.

A voice said, 'Don't move!' A man stepped out of the car and he was holding a gun. 'Who are you? What are you doing?' Strangers without clothes were dangerous, he had decided.

'Please, get the police, I said. I told him Kent Wagner's telephone number. 'I'm cold and very tired. If you telephone Captain Wagner, he'll come and get me.'

He took me inside the house and made me stand just inside the front doors. Still holding the gun, he put a hand through a doorway next to him and found a towel. He came across and put the towel around my waist, then he went to a telephone near the door. He asked me to repeat Wagner's telephone number. I did, and I told him my name.

Wagner was there and answered the phone.

'There's somebody here who says his name is Andrew Douglas,' the man began, then stopped as Wagner shouted at the other end. Then he said, 'What? Yes, OK.' And he gave me the phone. 'He wants to talk to you.'

Chapter Nineteen

Wagner came with some clothes. I dressed and told him my story, then I took him back to the tree. He looked at it for a moment, then we walked in the direction Giuseppe-Peter went earlier the day.

About fifty metres from the tree we saw an ordinary house, with lights on downstairs and curtains partly cl was a number on the outside. 5270. Instead of g walked along the edge of the trees to the road. W small hand radio.

'Turn around,' he said to his men in the police cars that were near. 'Go back to 45th Street, turn left, then turn left again into Cherrytree. Move slowly along there until you reach me. No – repeat – no noise.'

We waited. He watched me calmly in the moonlight.

'Your girl-friend will be happy to have you back,' he said.

'Alessia?'

'The jockey. She found it difficult to speak because of crying, but she says she loves you.'

'Does she?'

He smiled at my face. 'Good news, is it? She's still at the Regency hotel and says she won't leave until you're free.'

The police cars came and we got into the back of one of them. There were lists of rented houses and Wagner looked at them. He pointed to one line of writing: *5270 Cherrytree Street, 20016, Rented October 16 for 26 weeks. Rent paid.* I nodded. He got out of the car again and talked to his men, then a few minutes later we drove back in the direction of 5270. Two policemen were sent into the trees, ready to go in at the back of the house. The cars were parked away from the house, but also ready.

'You stay out of the house,' Wagner told me.

'No,' I said. 'I'm going in. Don't argue.'

A gun was in Wagner's hand. 'OK … I suppose,' he said. 'Ready?'

d one word: 'Go!'

tting through the darkness. Wagner breaking the glass in gh the kitchen, with two ght towards the stairs. I saw men were shooting the lock that way.

ne were open. I ran towards w, don't do that!' Then he ith me following.

modern
sed. There
ng closer, we
agner took out a

But his eyes didn't see me. They were open, but seeing nothing.

There was a tent in the room and Giuseppe-Peter was opening it. He turned round, and there was a gun in his hand. He pointed it, and there were two shots. My arm burned as one of them took off some of the skin. The second one went past my ear. Without pausing, Wagner shot him.

He fell on his back, and I went over to him. It was Wagner who went into the tent for Freemantle.

Pietro Goldoni – Giuseppe-Peter, as I would always think of him – looked at me. But his eyes didn't see me. They were open, but seeing nothing.

EXERCISES

Vocabulary Work

Look again at the 'Dictionary Words' in this book.

1 Look at the picture on page 18. What have the men got over their faces?

2 Look at the picture on page 51. What are the missing words in these sentences?

There are five ...... around the .... The ... are bent over their horses' necks.

3 Choose the right word for each definition.

root	listening device	rent	drug
shrine	officers	ransom	Madonna
victim	locker	burglar alarm	rope

a A very, very small church.

b Someone who is harmed by a criminal.

c Policemen who give orders to other policemen.

d The money a kidnapper asks for.

e A small cupboard with a lock.

f The money you pay for somewhere to live.

g Very strong, thick string.

h The part of a plant under the ground.

i A machine which rings a bell if it sees or hears a burglar.

j A very strong microphone.

k The Virgin Mary, Christ's mother.

l Something that makes you sleepy.

Comprehension

Chapters 1–3

1 Why was Andrew angry with the police in Bologna?
2 Who does Andrew *think* is the man who spoke to him in the motor-way café car park?

Chapters 4–6

3 Where did they find the ransom money?
4 Why did Alessia go to England?

Chapters 7–10

5 How did the kidnappers take Alessia to the hotel near Viralto?
6 Why was the boat burned on the beach?

Chapters 11–14

7 Why can't Nerrity pay the ransom money?
8 How did Tony bring Dominic out of the house?

Chapters 15–16

9 Why is it strange that Dominic said 'Ciaio bambino'?
10 Why does Giuseppe-Peter frighten Andrew?

Chapters 17–19

11 Look at the picture on page 55. What are the men doing to Andrew, and why?
12 How does Andrew escape?

13 There are some very rich people in this book. How do they, or their organisations, get rich?
14 Write about three occasions when someone in the book is in danger, and describe how they escaped.

Discussion

1 Read Chapter 3 again, and notice how Paolo Cenci is *feeling*. Now read the first two pages of Chapter 11 again, and notice how John Nerrity feels. How are the two men different? Why do you think this is?

2 Andrew didn't tell Eagler where the kidnappers were hiding Dominic. Why not? Was he right?

3 Pietro Goldoni agreed to change his ransom demand to the words Andrew suggested. Why do you think he agreed to do it?

Writing

1 Because Andrew is telling the story, nobody describes him. However, we know quite a lot about him from the pictures (pages 23, 51 and 55), by what he can do and what Alessia feels about him. Write about 75–100 words saying what he looks like and what kind of person he is.

2 Write a newspaper report about the kidnapping of Dominic Nerrity (100–150 words).

Review

1 Did you like Andrew Douglas? Say why you would like – or would not like – to read another book about him and his work.

2 The title doesn't tell you much about the book. Can you think of a better one? (NB You can't use *Kidnapped* since there's already a book with that title!)